T0171495

20 Things that Have to Materialize For the Proper Path To Marriage

*I.E. Doing It God's Way

Rev. Catherine Ross

WESTBOW
PRESS
A DIVISION OF THOMAS NELSON

Scripture taken from the King James Version of the Bible.
Scripture taken from the Holy Bible, New International Version®. Copyright © 1973, 1978, 1984 Biblica. Used by permission of Zondervan. All rights reserved.
Scripture quotations taken from the Holy Bible, New Living Translation, copyright 1996, 2004. Used by permission of Tyndale House Publishers, Inc., Wheaton, Illinois 60189. All rights reserved.

WestBow Press books may be ordered through booksellers or by contacting:

WestBow Press
A Division of Thomas Nelson
1663 Liberty Drive
Bloomington, IN 47403
www.westbowpress.com
1-(866) 928-1240

Because of the dynamic nature of the Internet, any web addresses or links contained in this book may have changed since publication and may no longer be valid. The views expressed in this work are solely those of the author and do not necessarily reflect the views of the publisher, and the publisher hereby disclaims any responsibility for them.

Any people depicted in stock imagery provided by Thinkstock are models, and such images are being used for illustrative purposes only.
Certain stock imagery © Thinkstock.

ISBN: 978-1-4497-6376-3 (sc)
ISBN: 978-1-4497-6377-0 (e)
Library of Congress Control Number: 2012914899

Printed in the United States of America

WestBow Press rev. date: 09/24/2012

In Appreciation

"To Rodney my husband - thank you for allowing me to be me and I love you dearly!"

"Dedicated in Loving Memory of Mary "Maria" Daniel - We miss you so much but know where you are at. Thank you for encouraging me to write and for believing in me. Without you and your husband Leonard, I wouldn't have been able to publish this. Thank you God for bringing both of you into our lives."

"To my family and especially my Mom: Mary Ann Conley, thank you for loving and encouraging me to write. Mom: "This Too Shall Pass" is still some the best advice I have gotten. Thank you."

"To Pastor Paul & Darla Mills, my "other" family, thank you for allowing two broken people to enter your world and for pouring your lives and the Love of God into ours. God Bless You!"

Foreword

*A*s a Pastor I have often thought, how *awesome* would it be to have a list of questions to help someone think through their futures. I believe this book is a <u>good start</u> in that process. The goal of this book is to get men and women to think about what you are committing to.

People get married for many reasons, a way out, a way up, loneliness, and many others. A person is not ready to be married until they are willing to be single. Rev. Catherine Ross has written this book to be a guideline requiring answers to many unasked questions. If time is taken and questions answered **truthfully** much pain and confusion can be avoided.

The question not asked is the most dangerous, so read this book, answer the questions *"truthfully"* and then ask and answer your own thoughtful questions.

Remember first we make choices and then our choices make us.

Senior Pastor Paul Mills

Faith Chapel

20 Things That Have To Materialize For The Proper Path To Marriage *I.E. Doing It God's Way

*T*his is dedicated to those of you who feel the call of God to be in a marriage that is God centered. This is to prepare you, and also possibly to move your current friendship to the next level. This is to prevent what I call: "Before Your Blue With I Do".

This list was given to me to answer some questions personally that I had about frustration in relationships. I was going through an examination of my life relationships and asked God where did I miss it? He explained to me that I had to have Him first in my life, as a priority (not lip service) and gave me this list of 20 Things; then expanded it to become this book you are holding. Each statement, question, and thought is coming from a person who has been broken into small pieces, because of life storms, some I created, some created for me by others choices. Each of the "20 Things" is something that I wished that someone had told me before I got married, it would have saved my husband and I a lot of time, frustration, and heartache. When I was ready to listen, my best friend, told this to me to heal me and to share with others so that we get this right.

I have enclosed something that I titled "Time Of Reflection" under each numbered item, and also a separate page by itself. This is to give you an opportunity to pray and seek God about each statement. Seek **His** will in all you read in this book and think upon each statement and question listed.

This is the order that God gave this to me, as I could accept each thought.

When looking for a mate recognize these qualities:

1. God is first in their life, there is no other relationships that are in the way of the ultimate relationship. They don't put anyone or anything in God's place. If Jesus is not 1st in their life, then the temptation will be to place the "potential marriage partner" in God's place. (This is very hard to overcome once it is done, however it is possible to change; you just have to address your motives in pursuing this relationship, and make the necessary changes to put Jesus first.) Jesus really is the best friend anyone could have as Lord and Savior. Lord meaning that He is in control of their lives and Savior meaning that they accepted the sacrifice and deliverance from the penalty of sin.

Scripture: *But seek ye first the kingdom of God, and his righteousness; and all these things shall be added unto you. Matthew 6:33*

Prayer: God as I seek you to be first in my life help me to keep you as the ultimate priority. You first God. Nothing and No one comes before you. And I thank you that my friend is doing the same in their life.

Time Of Reflection:

_____

_____

2. There is time invested in pursuit of you. They watch and study you and invest in a friendship first. In today's world this may sound strange, but If you are not a friend it will not be easy to maintain a marriage. What brought you two together should not only be God, but the friendship also. Attractions and sparks come and go; but the relationship that is vital to God and you will last.

Scripture: **Study** *to shew thyself approved unto God, a workman that needeth not to be ashamed, rightly dividing the word of truth. 2 Timothy 2:15*

(What does God's word say about this friendship)

*And the LORD spake unto Moses face to face, as a man speaketh unto his **friend**. Exodus 30:11*

Prayer: <u>God thank you for my friend. I praise you that you have brought this friendship/relationship together, please lead us to your plans as we seek to fulfill your ultimate purpose in our lives.</u>

Time Of Reflection:

_____

_____

3. They are tender hearted towards God. They are sensitive to His requests and listen closely. They don't repeatedly disobey the Holy Spirit. They show honor to the Holy things of God. They have

a heart to be pleasing to God in all that they do and say. (No lip service, but in words, and deeds). They know that obedience is better than sacrifice.

Scripture: *The fear of the LORD is the beginning of **wisdom**: and the knowledge of the holy is understanding. Proverbs 9:10*

Prayer: <u>God thank you that I want to be led by you in all things that pertain to this life. Help me to always be quick to obey and quick to repent and let me do the request right the first time you ask. And Lord I ask the same for my friend that you lead them as well.</u>

Time Of Reflection:

_____

_____

4. They are tender hearted towards you, they see you beyond what you are dealing with at the moment in the best of times and/or the worst of times. They see God's purpose and plan and help you to move forward. They don't consider all the negative circumstances that surround you at the moment.

Scripture: *...not realizing that God's **kindness** is intended to lead you to **repentance**? Romans 2:4b (NIV)*

Prayer: <u>God I am so grateful for the tenderness and kindness you have show me. Thank you that my friend operates in this tenderheartedness towards you and me.</u>

Time Of Reflection:

_____

_____

5. Love sparks come and go, but commitment stays. They are committed to the friendship in realms that others will not stay. Committed friends walk in and stay in when others walk out. Those that stay and believe in you and what you are called to do **they matter**. Those that stay to see you bleed, are not worth it. Learn to recognize who wants to see you struggle and tries to keep you in the struggle; instead of seeing and helping you to rise above the issues that you are dealing with.

Scripture: *One who has unreliable **friends** soon comes to ruin, but there is a **friend** who **sticks** closer than a brother. Proverbs 18:24 (NIV)*

Prayer: <u>Lord thank you that you are committed to me and you said that you would never leave me or forsake me. Thank you Lord that have made me to be committed to our friendship. Help me to stay focused and committed to you first and my friend to do the same.</u>

Time Of Reflection:

_____

_____

6. They are into the details that matter to you. If they disregard something that you absolutely love, first consider it a learning curve, then after showing you that they don't care about (for example) throwing trash out the window, that it is a priority to you; maybe you just need to embrace them as a **potential** friend. Make sure that you gently discussed what matters to you. Most of the time God brings complete opposites together. What you lack is found in them and what they lack is found in you. That is not what is being discussed here. **The action that is a blatant disregard of what you and your friend know that you have discussed and come to terms with, please note and pay attention to their response. If you have a detail that is not known to them that you need them to understand, then explain it to them.** I call this one of the love languages. Each relationship has a language to it. Someone who truly cares, will not casually disregard your "*understood*" love language.

Scripture: *Let all things be done **decently** and in order. 1 Corinthians 14:40 (NIV)*

(How things are going is it in order of God's desire?)

Rev. Catherine Ross

Prayer: <u>Lord thank you that what matters to me, matters to you and what matters to my friend, matters to you and me. Help me to see the areas that I need to grow in and help me to do the work necessary to make the changes. Please help my friend to do the same as we seek your ultimate will in our lives.</u>

Time Of Reflection:

_____

_____

7. They understand your purpose together. There has been some thought time with the Lord regarding the best interest in the "friendship". Each friendship has a purpose. Some encourage you, some embarrass you and some grow you and sometimes you go through all of this with the same friend.

Scripture: *For I know the plans I have for you," declares the LORD, "plans to prosper you and not to harm you, plans to give you hope and a future. Jeremiah 29:11 (NIV)*

Prayer: <u>Lord thank you that each of us has a purpose and you have a plan. Help us Lord to seek your will in all that is purposed for our lives and whether we are "together" or not.</u>

Time Of Reflection:

_____

_____

8. Their dreams align with God and flow for His purpose. If they are going in your direction you will have the consistent togetherness that occurs in friendships, it won't be a hard struggle to be together. It is important to know what is the possible marriage partner's dreams? Is it to open a local shop, when you are to go around the world, that will unfortunately make a lonely marriage and a potential divorce. You must be going in the same direction (Are you called into the ministry, Are they?)

Scripture: *Do two **walk** together unless they have **agreed** to do so? Amos 3:3*

Prayer: <u>God thank you that I walk in agreement with you today. That I don't dream, process or plan outside your purposes for my life. Thank you for the same for my friend.</u>

Time Of Reflection:

_____

_____

9. They have a mission statement of a life together. This means that they sought the Lord regarding your callings, gifts, talent and they want you in their future. A mission statement is to keep you and the possible marriage partner on the same page and once married on the same page continually.

Rev. Catherine Ross

Scripture: *My people are destroyed for lack of knowledge: because thou hast rejected knowledge. Hosea 4:6a*

Prayer: <u>God thank you for our mission statement: (Please put your life purpose together it goes here.) If you haven't received this step yet, then pray for your purpose to be fulfilled. *By the way you should be praying for your "God purpose" to be fulfilled, even they are in a training session with God.</u>

(Training sessions with God are those "things" that come up in our lives that we have to work on. (Traits, Habits, Opinions, Hurts, etc...). We have to allow God to heal us, in order to move forward.

Time Of Reflection:

_____

_____

10. This person believes in what God created you to be. They don't hold you back and they are excited about what God is doing through you. They see His potential and are helping you to get there. They don't walk in jealously and know that no matter what the outcome of the relationship is they are willing to help you.

Scripture: **Neglect not** *the gift that is in thee, which was given thee by prophecy, with the laying on of the hands of the presbytery. 1 Timothy 4:14*

Prayer: <u>God thank you that you help me to be the person that you see me as. I am the future that you created in me to be before I was in my mother's womb. And I thank you God for helping my friend be who they are called to be, with me or without me. Lead us Lord.</u>

Time Of Reflection:

_____

_____

11. They want you to succeed alongside them. They want the blessings to flow not only to you, but through both of you so you both are stronger.

Scripture: ***Iron*** *sharpeneth* ***iron****; so a man sharpeneth the countenance of his friend. Proverbs 27:17*

Prayer: <u>God thank you that you never leave me or forsake me, and even grant me with true friendships that see me succeeding. Thank you for the one that you placed in my life to succeed alongside. Give us wisdom and direction as to your timing and fulfilling our life purpose whether together or not.</u>

Time Of Reflection:

_____

_____

12. They have a drive to succeed but **will not run you over to do it**. (***Pay close attention here***). Sometimes you are the one in the lead and then

something's in life snags and you can feel left behind. They are the one pulling for you but will not run you over if you have to repeat some training that God is doing in you.

Scripture: *The **steps** of a good man are **ordered** by the LORD: and he delighteth in his way. Psalm 37:23*

***Order** my **steps** in thy word: and let not any iniquity have dominion over me. Psalm 119:133*

Prayer: <u>God thank you that you push me when I need it and that you let me learn what I need to know when you believe that I can process it. Thank you for Godly friendships that do the same.</u>

Time Of Reflection:

_____

_____

13. They have family connections that are there. Some families are supportive, some are not. But you should never be cut off from family in the sense that you don't have a relationship with them. It may not be perfect but you still love them. Remember the friend and how they treat their mom is how they will treat you. See that example. And how they respect their dad is how they will respect you. Cut a little slack for someone who has be in abusive situations. They need to work through it and they need God's deliverance. *You don't want them to bring in baggage from the past into this possible

marriage commitment. If ties are cut from the original family (and that happens to benefit all) they still need a spiritual family. Check to see if they have good connections there. If they do, great. See how they interact and look for growth, knowledge and wisdom of the spiritual family. If they don't have those connections that is your clue to remember that friendship (just for now, possibly) is the road to take. Consider introducing them to a spiritual family that could help them and watch them grow.

Scripture: *Honour thy father and thy mother: that thy days may be long upon the land which the Lord thy God giveth thee. Exodus 20:12*

Prayer: <u>Lord you placed me in a family to be loved and to love. If they didn't fulfill your purpose in that for me, Lord I forgive them. I want to have close relationships in a family structure that I don't have right now, bring me to a place where I can heal and grow.</u>

(If you have a spiritual family)

<u>And I want to thank you for my spiritual family who loves me and connects with me regularly.</u>

<u>Lord I pray for my friend that they are able to move forward in this family connections as well.</u>

Time Of Reflection:

_____

_____

14. This person will love what you love. And you love what they love. They get excited about what you love. You get excited about what they love. You will have like passions and be able to grow in Christ with the passion of the things you love. (Love animals, they do too, Love to help people, they do too. Love to see new things, they do too. Love to see lives changed, they do too.)

Scripture: *Do two **walk** together unless they have **agreed** to do so? Amos 3:3*

Prayer: God thank you that you use what I love and what my friend loves to keep us connected together. Thank you for leading this friendship and directing our steps. Let us continue to grow in Christ and in this friendship whether it grows into a potential marriage or not.

Time Of Reflection:

_____

_____

15. They are compassionate yet, can look beyond the current moment and help you refocus on God. They don't see the crying fit you just had as a note to step away, they see the breakdown as a place to grow from. Anything that comes against you, they may feel it come against them and they want to fight for you in prayerful ways to help you overcome.

Scripture: *But God commendeth his love toward us, in that, while we were yet sinners, **Christ died** for us. Romans 5:8*

Prayer: <u>Lord, while I was at my worst, you saw the best in me. Thank you for loving me and for your sacrifice. Thank you for the friendship, that we see the best in each other and know that the worst moments are temporary.</u>

Time Of Reflection:

_____

_____

16. Committed to the marriage bed. You only. If they cannot consider dating you only, then <u>move on</u>. If they cannot be only for you then they will be divided towards you. A friend is a friend and it is important to have them, but a path to committed marriage is only for you and that person only. No one else is to be on the side or in the background.

Scripture: *What therefore God hath **joined together**, let not man put asunder. Mark 10:9*

Prayer: <u>God thank you that you only are God of my life, just like me putting you first in my life, my friendship with .... Has progressed to pursuit of marriage, and Lord I want to thank you that we are focused on you and as we grow close to you, we grow</u>

closer together. Thank you that we are becoming the married couple that you desire of us.

Time Of Reflection:

_____

_____

17. They will be helping you to reach out to others and not be jealous. You have gifts, talents and abilities that others need in their lives. They pray and believe for open doors for you and sometimes they push you through them.

Scripture: *And the lord said unto the servant, Go out into the highways and hedges, and **compel** them to come in, that my house may be filled. Luke 14:23*

Prayer: Lord thank you that when you compel me to do something it is for my betterment. Thank you for helping my friend in their betterment as well.

Time Of Reflection:

_____

_____

18. They have a compassionate heart for your "lost" family members. They want to see your family in the Kingdom of God. And will pray and believe with you regarding that.

Scripture: *And they said, Believe on the Lord Jesus Christ, and thou shalt be saved, and thy house. Acts 16:31*

Prayer: <u>God thank you that my heart is fixed on seeing my friend's family being saved, healed and delivered. Lord you love them so much and your desire is that they not only know you but are known by you as true believers in Christ.</u>

Time Of Reflection:

_____

_____

19. They dream with you not against you. When they ask God for direction regarding where the relationship should go, they go by His leading and timing and they see you in their future. It does not matter what is thrown at them from the world, they cannot get you out of their mind. Also, they don't look for ways to exclude you in their life.

Scripture: *Do two **walk** together unless they have **agreed** to do so? Amos 3:3*

Prayer: <u>Father thank you that you don't exclude me in your plans for this world. I am grateful that I am not excluded in my friends plans for our life together as we serve you fully.</u>

Time Of Reflection:

_____

_____

20. They have your bests interests at heart. Not always wanting their way. They seek to serve you and want what is best for you. A friend who is operating in this is priceless, as most want what they can get from you. Also, note that you want to serve them and want what is best for them. One of the worst feelings in the world is to want to serve but you don't have an opportunity to do so.

Scripture: *Beloved, I wish above all things that thou mayest prosper and be in health, even as thy soul prospereth. 3 John 2*

Prayer: Lord thank you that your best interests were for me to be and do as you desire. Lord I thank you that I have a relationship that truly wants to serve me and I want to serve them. And in serving one another we help to fulfill your ultimate purpose for the Kingdom of God.

Another prayer: Lord, thank you that you see the best interests for this friendship and you see what I cannot. Help my friend and I to receive what is BEST for that is your ultimate desire.

Time Of Reflection:

_____

_____

_____

_____

_____

_____

_____

_____

_____

_____

_____

_____

_____

_____

_____

_____

_____

_____

_____

_____

_____

_____

Time Of Reflection

Comments to
Think Upon

I have heard that good is thief of what is best. The best is God's ultimate for your life and please hear me .. **don't settle**. Relationships take time to figure out where they belong in your life, and if you get in a big hurry, you **will** have a big mess.

I felt that the Holy Spirit gave this to me as to save you and your friendships from serious heartache. Nothing is worst than you feeling a certain way and thinking that your friend does too, but then finding out that they did not. Pains can be avoided if we learn to listen to the Holy Spirit. He is the Spirit of Truth and will lead you if you let him. Stay in the Spirit and you will NOT fulfill the lust of the flesh.

*(This I say then, Walk in the Spirit, and ye shall not fulfill the **lust** of the flesh. Galatians 5:16)*

If you messed up a relationship, and whether or not it has ended, you need to let go of the mistakes, forgive yourself, forgive them and move on. Past hurts always hold you back. **They are keeping you in bondage and you cannot freely move forward with chains of regret or bitterness clinging to you. (or the sayings of: I should have, could have or would have). LET IT GO.**

*T*his is for those who may have received this book by a relative or friend and you honestly don't feel like you are called to be a married person. I wanted to let you know that that **is ok**. (Please give the book to someone who feels God is calling it for them. Thanks!) God didn't call all of us to be married and you may feel some repulse from the opposite sex. Don't let the enemy confuse you into thinking that you need someone of the same sex or that you are just plain weird because you don't want to be married. It may not be your timing for marriage. You may have to release hurts or past experiences or harmful activities (drugs, alcohol, risky behaviors, etc...) before you can move forward. You may have things that you need to accomplish before you can think about these things. You are NOT weird. The enemy has used this knowledge of being single to make others think that if I don't like the opposite sex, then maybe I'm...gay? Don't entertain that thought or open that door. When the thought is entertained the enemy of your soul, will present "opportunities" for you to view things not as God sees them, but in a **Worldly Way** of thinking that **contradicts** the **Bible**. Being a believer of Jesus, means that we follow his ways and his complete word. The Bible is very clear that to be alone is fine and preferred and a gift to serve Him more fully. God created some to serve HIM fully with no division in their hearts of spouses and children.

Scripture:

Now concerning the things whereof ye wrote unto me: It is good for a man not to touch a woman.

2 Nevertheless, to avoid fornication, let every man have his own wife, and let every woman have her own husband.

3 Let the husband render unto the wife due benevolence: and likewise also the wife unto the husband.

4 The wife hath not power of her own body, but the husband: and likewise also the husband hath not power of his own body, but the wife.

5 Defraud ye not one the other, except it be with consent for a time, that ye may give yourselves to fasting and prayer; and come together again, that Satan tempt you not for your incontinency.

6 But I speak this by permission, and not of commandment.

7 For I would that all men were even as I myself. But every man hath his proper gift of God, one after this manner, and another after that.

8 I say therefore to the unmarried and widows, it is good for them if they abide even as I.

9 But if they cannot contain, let them marry: for it is better to marry than to burn. 1 Corinthians 7:1-9.

The Pharisees also came unto him, tempting him, and saying unto him, Is it lawful for a man to put away his wife for every cause?

4 And he answered and said unto them, Have ye not read, that he which made them at the beginning made them male and female,

5 And said, For this cause shall a man leave father and mother, and shall cleave to his wife: and they twain shall be one flesh?

6 Wherefore they are no more twain, but one flesh. What therefore God hath joined together, let not man put asunder.

7 They say unto him, Why did Moses then command to give a writing of divorcement, and to put her away?

8 He saith unto them, Moses because of the hardness of your hearts suffered you to put away your wives: but from the beginning it was not so.

9 And I say unto you, Whosoever shall put away his wife, except it be for fornication, and shall marry another, committeth adultery: and whoso marrieth her which is put away doth commit adultery.

10 His disciples say unto him, If the case of the man be so with his wife, it is not good to marry.

11 But he said unto them, All men cannot receive this saying, save they to whom it is given.

12 For there are some eunuchs, which were so born from their mother's womb: and there are some eunuchs, which were made eunuchs of men: and there be eunuchs, which have made themselves eunuchs for the kingdom of heaven's sake. He that is able to receive it, let him receive it. Matthew 19:3-12

The ABSOLUTE last thing I would want to do is make you feel guilty for relationship mistakes made or for not being married, or for not being in a relationship. You get enough of that nonsense from those who care about you, but may NOT understand you. No matter what, you are a gift from God

Lo, children are an heritage of the Lord: and the fruit of the womb is his reward. Psalm 127:3

and he does have a purpose for your lives, married or not. **Embrace the purpose**.

For I know the plans I have for you, declares the LORD, plans to prosper you and not to harm you, plans to give you hope and a future. Jeremiah 29:11

Questions To Consider Before Going Out The Door On A Date Or To Continue Dating This Friend

I thought I was finished with the 20 Things Book about moving a relationship into marriage. The more I thought about it the more I realized that we need to ask ourselves questions before we walk out the door to go on a date or to continue to pursue a relationship. **Consider these topics for you to look at and talk to only God about. Spend time in prayer seeking His face to help you.** The last thing you want to do on a first date is to have these out in the open to discuss with your date because you are not in relationship to have these discussions. And remember a relationship begins when you are the only one in that dating relationship with them.

Does this person really believe in Jesus Christ as Lord and Savior of their life? Do they exhibit His characteristics, traits, and does this person want me to draw closer to Him (meaning Jesus).

_____

_____

Do I have more than an attraction/sparks to this person?

_____

_____

Do I like their personality? Their humor?

_____

_____

Has this person ever display emotions in front of you? (Happy, Sad, Mad, or Anger) How do you feel about the emotions? (Does it scare you, make you upset, disappointed, Do you have too many expectations for them?)

_____

_____

Does this person have a reputation for being a hot head, have bitterness, or in resentment? Do I want to be around a person like that? Is that a true assessment of this person?

_____

_____

Have you met or seen an ex of theirs. (Friends, Marriage Partner or (s))? What do I think of that? (Do you know that they are an "ex" or did they just introduce them as a friend? How many "ex"s do they have? Am I ok with this?

_____

_____

How are you perceived by those closest to them? (A thrill ride {Something Temporary}, a nice person {Just A Friend}, a goldmine to cherish {Worth The Investment Of Their Time})?

_____

_____

Am I embarrassed by what they do, or by what affiliations that they have? (business, church, organizations, clubs, activities).

_____

_____

Do they make me want to be a better person? (Not in trying to win their approval but in the sense that just being around them, you want to do more and be more)

_____

_____

Have they any connections to anyone you know? Have they dated any of your family or extended family members, friends, etc… How do you feel about that? Have my friends past relationships ended good with the party that I know of?

_____

_____

Is there others (Friends, Family, etc…) in their life that don't approve of you? How much influence do they have in this one's life? How does this make you feel?

_____

_____

Does the friends/family **like you or make fun of you**? Do you want to pursue this relationship?

_____

_____

When you look at this person, do you feel excited to see them, or do you dread it? Why? (Be honest here, just being lonely and wanting "someone" is not going to cut it and it will end up with a lot of hurt feelings)

_____

_____

If you weren't able to see with your eyes, what is it that draws you to them, time and time again? Or is there anything to draw you to them?

_____

_____

Am I embarrassed of their past? If so, why? (Remember, God has delivered you from something) Is their past situation a deal breaker?

_____

_____

Are they going in the direction that God is telling me to go into?

_____

_____

Do we have any like passions?

_____

_____

Do we have any common interests?

_____

_____

What would a date look like? Where would we go?

_____

_____

What does my mom, dad, spiritual mom, or dad, brother, etc… think of this person? Does this matter to me? And I am acting in rebellion about that?

_____

_____

If the date was announced on the news as camera's flashed on would I be embarrassed or would I be overjoyed? (Learned this question in college … If it was on the nightly news would you do this?)

_____

_____

Does this person value my time with them? Do I value theirs?

_____

_____

Where does God want this to go? I have heard it said that if you don't think you will marry this person, don't spend time with them, as they could be the one to lead you astray from God's ultimate purpose. Would you consider marrying this individual why or why not?

_____

_____

What are your moral absolutes? (No drinking, no drugs, no sex before marriage, etc...) Does this person respect you and are they currently participating in these activities? IF so, why are you pursuing this relationship? What does God's word say about these things? Am I trying to please this person or God?

_____

_____

Has this person ever asked me or have I asked this person to dress more revealing? Why did this occur? Are they trying to compensate for lack (Of Self Esteem, Resources, Finances etc...) in their life by showing you off or are you trying to do the same?

_____

_____

What did it take to ask you out? Or did you ask them out?

_____

_____

How much time am I willing to invest in this friendship/ relationship? Do I honestly have the time to pursue this?

_____

_____

Have I had other conversations that lead me to believe what they want out of life, before going on this date? Why or why not?

_____

_____

If you have a close relationship to your Pastor, does the Pastor approve of this? What is their opinion?

_____

_____

Have I had any prophetic words spoken over me regarding being cautious about dating, friendships? Am I ignoring God's leading? (Note a prophetic word is about something that God has spoken to you (normally) and that is confirmed through another in the operation of the gifts of the Holy Spirit

_____

_____

(For to one is given by the Spirit the word of wisdom; to another the word of knowledge by the same Spirit. 1 Corinthians 12:8)

and it witnessed to your spirit. No one but the Holy Spirit can witness to your spirit.

_____

_____

Is this person in rebellion? Do they have close personal friends in rebellion?

_____

_____

Does this person have a lot of strife in their life? If so, why? Is their family in strife? Do they walk in Peace?

_____

_____

Have I seen or heard of this person ever being mean to an elderly person, a child or an animal? (If it was a long time ago, and they have either grown up from teen years or went to counseling, how do you feel about that?)

_____

_____

Do I like their family? If they have children, do I want to be around them? Do their children like you?

_____

_____

Did the person explain that they had children before pursuing you?

_____

_____

Would you consider a package deal? Meaning that you get the individual and their children? Is this a deal breaker for you?

_____

_____

Is this person only going out with me so I will buy their children something? Or Am I asking this from someone? What do I think of this behavior?

_____

_____

How am I perceive by the individuals children? Do they see me as a potential (Step-Mother if you are the lady, or Step-Father if you are the man). How do you feel about that? How is their relationship with the biological parent?

_____

_____

Do they always want to go shopping with you? Who pays? What is my opinion of this, is it a way for them to get me to buy them something?

_____

_____

Has this person ever expressed that they wanted you to buy them something (not in who pays for the date ((Men you really should be the one to pay for the date))). But did the person want you to buy them something or even to pay for something that is not normally something you would do for a friend? (Expensive items, repairs, expensive gifts)?

_____

_____

Is this person somewhat shallow or shy? Do they want to spend time with you or just show you off, in the sense of they are "not" alone and look who they are dating?

_____

_____

If this person is a "work in progress" in losing the shallowness, or are they dating you to make them feel good about themselves or for seeking approval from others, or are they really into you?

_____

_____

If the date went great yet, they weren't into you, how you feel about it?

_____

_____

If they date went awkward, yet you knew there was something there, are you willing to pursue it further?

_____

_____

Is this person a friend and if so, what if it didn't work out, how would you feel? How would this affect in your relationship? Work? Ministry?

_____

_____

Is this person a friend and if so, what if it **did** work out, how would you feel? How would this affect in your relationship? Work? Ministry?

_____

_____

Is this person your boss? What if this relationship did work out, is this going to cause strife at work? What if this didn't work out?

_____

_____

Is this person your direct subordinate? What if this relationship did work out, is this going to cause strife at work? What if this relationship didn't work out? Also, are you breaking any company policy by dating? Do you have to let someone know?

_____

_____

Has the person ever dated anyone at your work? If so, how did it end?

_____

_____

Does this person have a reputation for lovin' them and leavin' them? Is this a true assessment, if so why are you pursuing this relationship?

_____

_____

Is this person seeing someone else and trying to see you? How do you feel about that? Would you want to pursue this further? Why or Why not?

_____

_____

Have I defined what my moral absolutes (principles) are? Has this person ever pushed me into not having my moral absolutes (principles) or tried to push themselves on me?

_____

_____

If this person is seeing someone else, is this in your best interests? (remember these questions are to get you to think before you leap)

_____

_____

Does this person have manners? If so, can you improve on yours? What if they don't have the kind of manners you desire? Do they want to have manners? (Manners, guys open doors, ladies, allow man to open doors, there is more to it than this, but you know what you are comfortable with and if you never experienced it look up some info on it).

_____

_____

How has this person responded to ... you fill in the blank here as to what is important to you.

_____

_____

1. How I dress? Did their face light up to see me or are they embarrassed?

_____

_____

2. My feelings? Have I said or expressed something that they responded to? What was their reaction? (Be honest here, it will save you time, if you cried, did they tell you to be quiet or try to console you, if they consoled you was it genuine?)

_____

_____

3. Something about my body? (Did they look in disgust about some feature about your body? Do they try to hide their disgust about your nose, hair, feet, chin, etc...) Is that someone I want to be around?

_____

_____

Have they made fun of your features? If so, how did it make you feel? Have they looked away with a smile, to protect their eye gate? (in other words, they are attracted to you, but don't want to focus on a feature as they don't want to open the door to lust). Or are they looking away as they see you as a distraction?

_____

_____

If this person is one that tries to protect their eye gate (what they see), do I see it from a respect point of view? Or does it annoy me?

_____

_____

Do I want to kiss this person, if so, when would it be appropriate?

_____

_____

Learning When To Say When…

What if they want more from you in a physical way than you can offer? Let's say on the first date they have already held your hand, do you want to start off kissing on the first date? What if you just want your hand held first for awhile? Does a kiss on the cheek for a good night seem alright to you? If so, or if not why? Or Do you want a nice friendly hug? (Not pressing on you, just friendly) Does this person feel the same way you do about these things? Where is your boundary?

_____

_____

Let's say that you go on a first date and it was great, they held your hand, they gave you a hug goodnight. They call you up and you go out again, they hold your hand, and then they want to make out on the couch, where is the progression to start for you. Sex before marriage is prohibited, for any child of God, what is sex and how do you define it? Where is it located in the word of God?

_____

_____

Do you have a strategy for the pull of desiring this one in a more physical way? How do you protect the reputation of yourself and this individual? What is my exit strategy and does the other party have one for themselves as well? Is there a key phrase that lets them know that you or maybe them need to cool down and refocus as to not pursue this "relationship" in a physical way.

Let's say that the "relationship" is pursuing marriage and you know that eventually you "will" get married, what is your exit strategy to let the other party know that you are attracted to them, but you need to cool off?

Your Eyes Wide Open...

*I*f I am older/younger than this person what are my expectations about this relationship? Is this going anywhere? Am I embarrassment to them? Are they to me? What do others think of this and do you care?

What if the person has had attractions to the same sex and have moved on? In other words, they don't practice it and they don't look for it. Is this something that you are going to look over?

Am I willing to be there for this individual no matter what?

Has this person just gotten out of a major relationship? Are they ready for a person like me? Am I ready for them?

Is this person trying to compare me to another individual from their past? Do they try to encourage me to dress like someone else? (Why not wear scarves, my .... Used to wear ... and it looked great)

_____

_____

What does the person see in me that makes them want to go out with me? (Some are out for **the kill {They want to use you}**, some are out for **the look {They only go out with you because you look good or they are lonely and you look ok to them}**, and some just want **something real for a while {They are just lonely and want someone to do things with}**, and some are looking for **something real for a lifetime, {They are wanting a relationship that will lead to marriage}**).

_____

_____

Does this person have commitment issues? Do I have commitment issues? A person who is not committed to be alone with God for a "season", will not be able to be committed to you. If they have to have "someone" in their life, they will move to the next one either while you are together, just starting out or when the opportunity presents itself. **(Be wise and Be patient, Don't Settle!)**

_____

_____

Have they let go of their past? Or are they still hurting? How do I feel about that? Do I need to wait for them to heal before pursuing this further?

_____

_____

Am I ready to go out on a date? Do I have something to let go of? If so, what is holding me back?

_____

_____

Am I wanting to go out on a date, just because I am lonely? not because I am interested in this person? Why would I allow my loneliness to encourage me to be around someone I don't really want to be around?

_____

_____

Am I ok, to be alone? Do I enjoy being by myself? If I don't why would I think that someone else would enjoy being around me? Have I pursued Godly friendships and looked for ways to serve God in other ways? (Such as: helping an elderly person, taking in a pet from the shelter, reading to increase my knowledge of things, etc...)?

_____

_____

Have I ever seen this person, when they didn't look, smell, or feel their best? Did it gross me out? Were they sick? How did I respond to them?

_____

_____

Does this person want me in their life? Or do they need me in their life? Or is it both?

_____

_____

Is this person a leader in my church, Am I ready for controversy if we start pursuing a dating relationship? What if I am the leader? Have I sought Godly counsel about this?

_____

_____

If I am in ministry, is this person going to go with me, to minister? If so, why or why not? How do I protect our reputations in the dating process? Have I sought Godly counsel on this? Do our ministries go together?

_____

_____

Do we go to the same church? Am I willing to move to their church? Or are they willing to move to mine? Have I sought Godly counsel regarding this?

_____

_____

What are the needed rules for this dating relationship and are they wanting to abide by them? Do they understand the rules, or have I explained them to the individual in clear concise manner?

_____

_____

Does this person embarrass me in ministry? Have they ever said or did something to question yours or their integrity? Did I forgive them? Did I let it go? What does God say about this?

_____

_____

When people look at us together do they see us **together** or just **two individuals who are lonely**? (Really only a true friend can answer this question for you, make sure it's not from a friend who is a "yes" person. But make sure it is from someone who hears from God and will tell you the truth, whether they personally agree or not?)

_____

_____

Does this person make me think clearer or foggy?
(When around them, do you get fresh vision, direction,
clarity or just foggy feelings?)

_____

_____

If this person died today, how would I feel? How
would I explain how much they meant to me? Or do
they mean "that much to me"?

_____

_____

Has this person the same depth of feelings as I do?
Or are they just shallow? (Be Honest here, it will save
you time and heartache).

_____

_____

What would draw me closer to this individual if they
lost all their resources, finances, possessions, or had
lost all their hair, teeth, or other things?

_____

_____

What would happen if you found out that certain
items were missing from their body, or they had
medical issues such as a loss of a leg, a foot, or
they are paralyzed? Do you still want to pursue this

relationship? Are you intrigued by what happened? Do you feel pity? Or **are you just drawn to them by who they are**?

_____

_____

Are you wiling to learn what their needs are medically if the case above were true?

_____

_____

Do they have any medical needs that I need to be aware of? Is there training or other knowledge that I need to assist them?

_____

_____

Am I prejudice? Is my family? Is there cultural differences in our families?

_____

_____

Do I know how to love someone that could be a nuisance to others? (Maybe they have oddities or other quirks that are not known to others) Do I want to pursue this relationship?

_____

_____

Do I know my own quirks and how do they respond
to mine?

_____

_____

What is it I want to discover about this individual?
Their mind? Their humor? Their capacity for love?

_____

_____

Being Real Is Not Easy, But Necessary!

W hat if this person had a sexually transmitted disease, and you were not able to get too close until a true commitment of marriage (i.e. walk down the aisle, in front of witnesses, etc...) was made, are you willing to put yourself through that? Do others know of their condition? Have they ever knowingly transmitted the disease to someone? Is it currently transmittal to you? What precautions are needed? What counseling have I sought to know if this is what you feel God is calling you to?

_____

_____

_____

_____

_____

What precautions are you taking to make sure that this is right for you? Are **Your** eyes wide open?

_____

_____

_____

_____

_____

Do you believe in healing, does the other party believe like you do? What does God's word say about healing?

_____

_____

_____

_____

_____

Has this individual ever put you in harms way? Why is that NOT ok?

_____

_____

_____

_____

_____

Has this person ever knowingly done something to someone that could cause sickness, death? Have they been in jail, prison or in a other type of facility? Did this person pay the time for the crime? Have they given you reasons to believe the positive change in their life? Do they have family, friends that know who they were and who they are today and have seen the changes? Do you trust their opinions of the change? Does my friend have a mental illness? If the individual has a mental illness, do they take medicines and are they faithful to take them?

_____

_____

_____

_____

_____

*G*ranted some of these questions are to ask yourself in the path of relationship working on the assumption (yes assumption) that you just didn't meet this person and just say yes to go out, based on looks or sparks. Sparks come and go and honey, looks can fade fast. What looked good one moment can look bad in the light.

Also, keep in mind this is your discovery of what is God's best interest for you. You may have all the "feelings" for it, but when the feelings go you will need these questions answered in your mind.

Being willing and able to love someone is a gift from God, and being able to stay in relationship with them is another gift that has yet to be fulfilled.

Remember each time you walk out the door to a date, ask yourself, God did I go through the thought processes to make sure I am not jumping out ahead of you.

You need to be ready to date. Maybe not today, But someday you will, again, if you are called to be in a relationship (that leads to marriage).

Process each question and make up some of your own, this will determine where you are at in your walk with God and with relationship minded individuals.

Don't waste time with those who you will not marry… it's a dessert best not eaten and a distraction, best not observed.

Blessings to You!

If you would like to schedule Rev. Catherine Ross for your church meeting or event, please contact:

Faith Chapel

510 Summit Ave.

Arlington, TX 76013

www.arlingtonfaithchapel.org